Honesty is the Best Policy

OM KIDZ

An imprint of Om Books International

One day, a woodcutter was cutting wood in the forest. It was very hot and the sun beat down harshly on him.

"Oh, I'm so thirsty!" the woodcutter exclaimed. "Let me go drink water from the river nearby."

The woodcutter made his way to the river, carrying his axe. But in his haste to drink water, his axe accidentally slipped from his grasp and fell into the river.

"Oh no!" the woodcutter exclaimed. "My axe is gone! I must look for it!"

The woodcutter searched in the river for a long time, but could not find his precious axe.

"How shall I earn my livelihood now?" the woodcutter said in despair as he sat near the riverbank. Then, he started crying loudly. His sobs echoed throughout the forest.

Hearing him cry, an angel emerged from the river and stood before him.

"What is wrong, my good man?" the angel asked the woodcutter. "Why are you crying?"

The woodcutter sobbed louder now and the angel once again asked him what the matter was.

"My axe has fallen into the river!" the woodcutter said, between sobs.

"Don't worry!" the angel assured him. "I shall fetch it for you!"

The angel dived underwater and soon emerged, carrying a golden axe.

"Here is your axe!" the angel said to the woodcutter as she offered him the golden axe. But the honest woodcutter refused to accept the axe. After all, it did not belong to him.

"No, no!" he replied. "That is not my axe. My axe is made of iron, not gold!"

"It appears that I have made an error," the angel replied. "Let me try and find your axe again," the angel said and dived underwater again.

This time, the angel returned with another beautiful axe. This one was made of silver.

"Here's your axe!" the angel smiled at the woodcutter and handed him the silver axe.

"You've made a mistake again," the woodcutter said to the angel. "My axe is not made of gold or silver. It is an ordinary axe made of iron and wood. I use it to cut trees."

The angel smiled and dived underwater for the third time. This time the angel returned with the woodcutter's axe and he started jumping with joy on seeing his precious iron and wood axe.

"I believe this axe belongs to you!" the angel said to the delighted woodcutter.

"Yes, yes! That is my axe!" the woodcutter exclaimed happily as he thanked the angel again and again for having been so kind to find his axe.

"I am impressed by your honesty, my good man!" the angel stated. "Any other man would have taken the golden axe or the silver axe, but you didn't. Please accept all the three axes as a reward for being honest and truthful," the angel said as she handed the woodcutter the golden, the silver as well as his own axe.

The angel then returned underwater after the woodcutter had thanked her again. The woodcutter couldn't believe his luck! Not only had he found his own axe but was also the proud owner of a golden and a silver axe.